FUN ON THE RUN

Travel Games and Songs

by **Joanna Cole and Stephanie Calmenson**

with **Michael Street**

illustrated by **Alan Tiegreen**

A BEECH TREE PAPERBACK BOOK • NEW YORK

Portions of this book first appeared in
The Rain or Shine Activity Book: Fun Things to Make and Do and
Why Did the Chicken Cross the Road?: And Other Riddles Old and New

Printed in the United States of America.

1 3 5 7 9 10 8 6 4 2

First Beech Tree Edition, 1999
ISBN 0-688-14662-7

Library of Congress Cataloging-in-Publication Data
Cole, Joanna.
Fun on the run: travel games and songs / by Joanna Cole and Stephanie Calmenson with Michael Street;
illustrated by Alan Tiegreen.
p. cm.
Summary: A collection of games and songs to enjoy while traveling, including word games, memory games,
license plate games, writing games, geography games, jokes, and riddles.
ISBN 0-688-14660-0
1. Games for travelers—Juvenile literature.   2. Children's songs—Juvenile literature.
[1. Games for travelers.   2. Games.   3. Songs.]
I. Calmenson, Stephanie.   II. Street, Michael.   III. Tiegreen, Alan, ill.   IV. Title.   V. Title: Travel games and songs.
GV1206.C65 1999   793.7—dc21   98-42245   CIP AC

CONTENTS

INTRODUCTION

Never never, ever ever go on a trip empty-handed. Always bring something to do. And why not something that's fun?

We've packed a whole lot of fun into this book. Open it and see if you agree. If you do, bring it along.

Have a good trip!

WORD GAMES

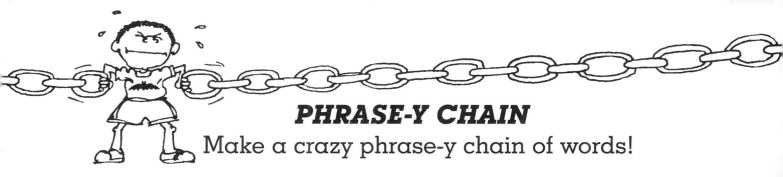

PHRASE-Y CHAIN

Make a crazy phrase-y chain of words!

1. The first player begins by naming a short, common phrase, such as "Lunch box."

2. The next player must say a phrase beginning with the last word of the first player's phrase. Here, she could say "Box spring." The phrases must be common and recognizable by other players. "Box giraffe" or "box green," for example, would not be acceptable phrases.

3. Play continues, with each player naming a phrase beginning with the last word of the phrase named by the previous player.

4. When a player cannot think of a phrase, he is out. When only one player remains, he is the winner!

Phrases can be of any length, but as you get better at the game, you might want to limit the number of words in a phrase. The fewer words you allow, the harder the game will get.

Another option is to try to bring the chain back to the beginning phrase. There is no winner, just a group effort to steer the phrases in the right direction. In the example above, the game might end with the phrases "spring break," "break free," "free lunch," and then "lunch box."

TWENTY QUESTIONS
Which one of your friends is the best detective?

1. Choose one player to be the leader. She must have in mind the name of an object or famous person for the other players to guess.

2. The other players take turns asking questions about the mystery word or name that can be answered "Yes" or "No." Good questions will build on the answers to previous questions. If players find out that the leader has chosen a person's name, they might try to determine if that person is alive or dead, a man or a woman, and what the person is famous for.

3. The first person to guess the mystery word correctly on or before the twentieth question is the leader for the next game. If no one can guess the mystery by the twentieth question, the leader chooses another mystery word, and the game begins again.

Twenty Questions usually begins with the question "Is it animal, vegetable, or mineral?" This is the only question allowed that cannot be answered "Yes" or "No." The mystery word is considered "animal" if it is a person or animal or if it comes from an animal. A lion, a doctor, and a leather briefcase are all "animal." The word is "vegetable" if it is some kind of plant or comes from a plant. A flower, a carrot, and a cotton shirt are all "vegetable." Everything else is "mineral." This includes anything made of stone, metal, or plastic. This first question will help players narrow down the possibilities and make the game a little easier to win.

GHOST
This game's scary only if you can't spell

1. The game begins when one player says a letter out loud. The next player adds a letter to this one, thinking of a word that begins with these two letters.

2. In turn, each person adds a letter to the end of the chain, as long as the new letter can still begin a longer word but does not yet complete a "legal" word. A legal word is any word that is found in a dictionary, or any name of a person or a place. When each player has given a letter, the game continues with the first player.

3. If a player adds a letter to the chain that doesn't sound like it could form part of a word, another player may challenge her letter. If she cannot name a word beginning with the letter chain that includes her letter, she is a ghost and out of the game. For example, if the first three letters are *B-U-L-*, and the next player says "*X*," another player may challenge the person who said "*X*." That player must then name a word beginning with *B-U-L-X-* (an impossible task, because there is no such word).

4. If the letter he says completes a word, that player is a ghost and out of the game. This is true even if the player finishes a shorter word in the process of spelling out a longer one. For example, if a player adds an *N* to *W-I-*, wanting to spell *WINDOW,* he has nonetheless finished the word *WIN* and is a ghost.

5. Once one player becomes a ghost, the letter chain begins again with the person following the ghost. Keep playing until one player is left. She is the winner!

For a longer game, try this variation. When a player makes her first mistake, she is not immediately out of the game. Instead of being a *GHOST*, she is just a G. After her second mistake, she is a *GH*, and a *GHO* after her third mistake. This continues until she is a *GHOST* and is out of the game.

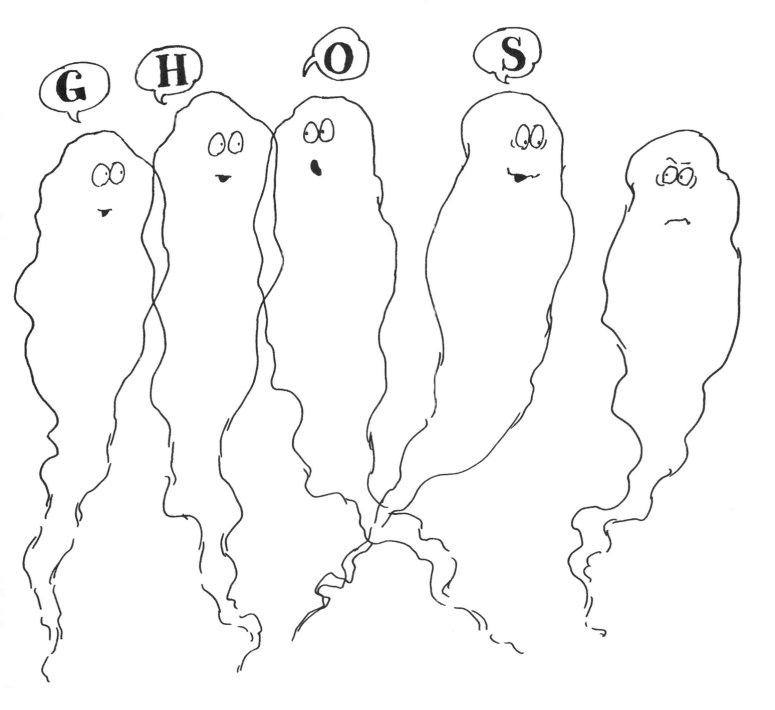

ALPHABET PAIRS

From "Apple Dumpling" to "Yapping Dog"—
can you get all the way through the alphabet?

1. The players agree on a key letter they will all use in their phrases—the letter *D*, for instance.

2. The first player names a common two-word phrase whose first word begins with *A* and whose second word begins with the key letter. For example, he might say "Apple Dumpling."

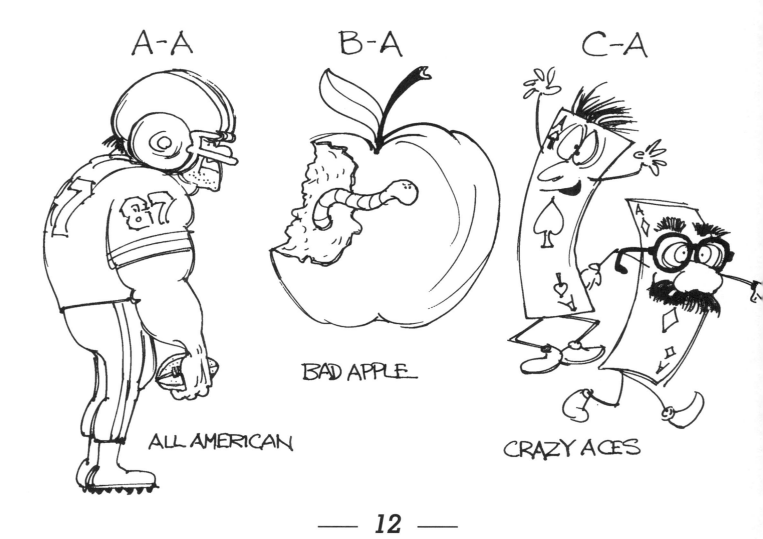

A-A
ALL AMERICAN

B-A
BAD APPLE

C-A
CRAZY ACES

3. The next player names a two-word phrase whose first word begins with *B* and whose second word begins with the key letter. She might say, for example, "Bad Dog." Phrases must be common and recognizable by other players. "Car Bargain" makes sense, but it's not a common phrase. "Coke Bottle" would be better.

4. Play continues through the alphabet, with the second word of the phrase always beginning with the key letter. Skip the letters *X* and *Z*.

5. The game ends when the players go all the way through the alphabet. If one player cannot think of a phrase when it is his turn, he may pass.

6. Pick a new key letter and start the game again!

Another option is to go through the alphabet using consecutive letters, instead of having the second word contain the same key letter. The first player names a phrase whose first word begins with *A* and second word with *B*, the second player names a *C-D* phrase, and so on.

Also, the game can be played competitively. When a player names an unacceptable phrase or cannot think of a phrase at all, she is out. The winner is the one player left, although it might take more than one trip through the alphabet with more than one key letter to determine a winner.

BOTTICELLI
Try and guess who I am!

1. The first player thinks of a famous person and tells the other players what the first letter of the person's last name is. For example, she might think of Marilyn Monroe and say, "My last name begins with *M*."

2. Players try to think of famous people whose last names begin with the chosen letter. They take turns asking the first player "stumper" questions based on the famous people they think of. The answer to the stumper questions must be a famous person whose last name begins with the same letter as the mystery person's. For example, a stumper question could be, "Are you a cartoon character?"

3. If the first player knows an answer to the stumper question, she says, "No, I'm not . . ." and gives the answer. In this example, she could answer, "No, I'm not Mickey Mouse."

4. If the first player does not know an answer to the stumper question, the player who asked the stumper question can ask her a yes-or-no question about the mystery person's identity, such as "Are you still alive?" or "Are you female?" The first player must answer truthfully.

5. Players continue asking stumper questions until a question is asked that the first player can answer only with the truth (either because there is no other possible answer or because no other answer comes to mind). The first player then says, "Yes, I'm Marilyn Monroe" (or whoever she chose), and the game is over.

6. The player who asked the final stumper question now thinks of a new mystery person, and the game begins again.

CELEBRITIES
No looking in the Hollywood phone book!

1. The first player begins by giving the full name of any celebrity.

2. The next player must name another celebrity whose first name starts with the same letter as the last name of the first player's celebrity. For example, if the first player names Michael Jordan, the second player might name Jack Nicholson.

3. The game continues in this way, with players taking turns naming celebrities.

4. When more than two people are playing, any celebrity with the *same* first and last initial reverses the direction of the game, so that the previous player must now name a new celebrity. For example, if player one says, "Joe Montana," player two says, "Mariah Carey," and player three says, "Charlie Chaplin," player two must now name a celebrity whose first name begins with C, and play then continues with player one.

5. If a player cannot name a celebrity, or says one who has already been named, she is out, and the game continues with the next player. The last person left is the winner!

You can make this game even more challenging by allowing only a certain kind of celebrity, such as authors, movie stars, or professional athletes.

TOM SWIFTIES

"You'll love this game," Tom said heartily

1. When Tom Swift talks, he uses adverbs that make a joke about what he says. These quotations are called "Tom Swifties" and are hilarious to make up and listen to. Here are some examples:

"I need to get to the other side of the street," Tom said crossly.

"I love trees," Tom said woodenly.

"I really don't like hot dogs," Tom said frankly.

"Would you like a piece of candy?" Tom asked sweetly.

2. All players must think up a "Tom Swifty" (or more than one!) and tell it to the other players. Everyone votes on the funniest one, and the player with the most votes is the winner.

WORDS FOR SALE
What would you pay for a RADIO?

1. The game begins when one player offers a word for sale, such as *radio*.

2. The other players "buy" the word by taking turns naming items, one beginning with each letter of the sale word. Try for ridiculous or uncommon words (you'll see why in a minute).

3. For RADIO, players might name Rutabaga, Abacus, Delicatessen, Igloo, and Orangutan. The player selling the word should write down the words that other players name.

4. The player selling the word then must make up a silly story using all the words given by the other players.

5. When her story is finished, another player offers a word for sale, and the game continues as before.

6. When everyone has "sold" a word and made up a silly story, the other players vote on whose story was the funniest. The player with the most votes is the winner.

ACRONYM SENTENCES
Game Requires Outrageous Sentence Skills

An acronym is a word formed from the initial letters of a phrase. For example, the word *scuba* is an acronym, formed from the phrase Self Contained Underwater Breathing Apparatus.

1. The first player names a word, and then every player makes an acronym of the word, by thinking up a sentence in which the first letter of each word spells out the first player's word.

2. For example, the word *color* might give you "Charlie Owes Larry Outrageous Rent." The sentences should be complete and make sense ("Coming Over Later On, Ralph" isn't a complete sentence, and "Corn Or Lard Observes Redness" doesn't make any sense).

3. When every player has come up with a sentence, each person says his out loud. After all players have said their sentences, everyone votes on the funniest, and the player with the most votes wins.

4. The winner then chooses a new word and the game begins again.

You can vote for different categories of sentences, like the one that makes the most sense, or require everyone to make up sentences only about people playing the game. You can also have people say their sentences as soon as they make them up; the fastest player (with a sentence that makes sense) is the winner.

DOG-BARK-TREE

"Wood" you like to try this clever
word association game?

1. The first player names a common word that has more than one meaning, such as *ship* (to send something, or a sailing vessel) and *bark* (part of a tree, or a sound a dog makes). Each of these words is a homonym—a word having the same spelling and pronunciation as another word or words but a different meaning. Other good words are *road/rowed* and *pair/pear*. These are homophones—words with the same pronunciation but different spellings and meanings.

2. The next player must name a word associated somehow with the first player's word. From the word *pear*, a player could name *berry* (another fruit).

3. Then the following player must name a word associated with a *different meaning* of the previous player's word. For example, if the game goes from *pear* to *berry*, the third player could say *two* (associated with *pair*). The fourth player could say *coffin* (associated with *bury*).

4. Play continues in this way, with the object being to keep the word chain going until one player is able to name the first word again. For example, if the game begins with *road* and continues with *oar* (associated with *rowed*), *conjunction* (associated with *or*), and so forth, the game could end when a player is given the word *race* and says *track* (as in *track and field*), which leads directly into a different meaning of *road*.

5. Once the chain has been completed—when a player names the first word again—another player begins with a new word and the game begins again.

6. Resist the urge to end the game after only five or six words. Challenge yourself to make the word association chain as long as possible!

Any player can challenge a word by asking the person who named it to explain the association. Challenging should be fun, not competitive, giving players a chance to show how clever their word choice is. In fact, Dog-Bark-Tree is meant to be a cooperative game, not a competitive one.

STORY CHAIN
What could possibly come next?

1. The first player starts by naming an object, preferably something very small. "I have the mayor's favorite cuff link," he might say.

2. The next player then adds to the description, naming something connected to the first player's object—for instance, "I have the shirt that holds the mayor's favorite cuff link."

3. Players take turns adding to the description: "I have the iron that pressed the shirt that holds the mayor's favorite cuff link" and "I have the cord to the iron . . . " and so forth.

This is a game that could easily become a kind of story. You can play it competitively, where the first person who can't think of something new is out, or cooperatively, where everyone works together to create a unique story.

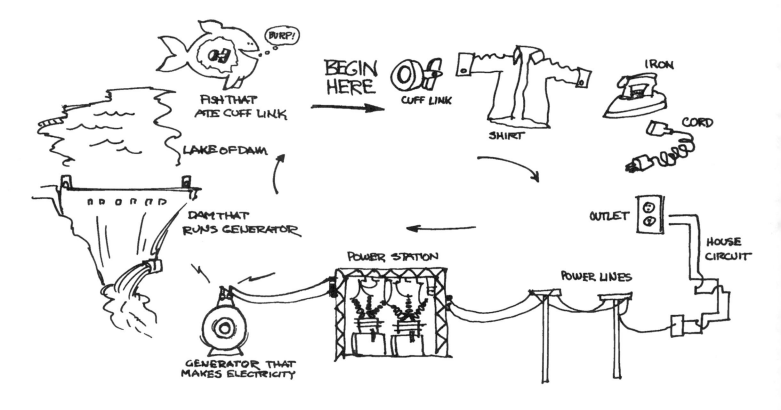

SOUNDS ALIKE
Can you get the homophone?

1. The first player thinks up a sentence with a pair of homophones. Homophones are words that sound alike, but have different spellings and meanings, like *sea* and *see* or *to, two,* and *too.*

2. Once the first player has thought up his homophone sentence, he gives a clue to the other players to help them guess it. For example, if his sentence is "He stares at the stairs," the clue might be "A boy looks at steps."

3. The other players try to guess the sentence. If there are more than two people playing, everyone can take turns trying to guess, or the first person to figure out the sentence can just guess it.

4. The player who figures out the sentence thinks up a homophone sentence of her own, and the game begins again.

DIAL-A-WORD

A fun 4263 for anyone who's ever used a 835374663

1. Each player should quickly draw (or write out) a telephone keypad, like the one below. Notice that there are no letters for the number 1.

2. One player thinks up a word and then figures out the telephone code, which is how she would "dial" it on the keypad. *Green* would be 47336.

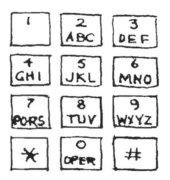

3. She then tells the other players what the telephone code for her word is. The other players try to figure out what the word is; this can be difficult, since each number stands for any of three letters.

4. The player who correctly guesses the first player's word thinks up a word of his own, and the game begins again.

The game can also be played in reverse! Write down a list of phone numbers that you call often—your home number, the work numbers of your parents, or the numbers of some of your friends. Try to figure out words that you can spell with these phone numbers. This is not only a lot of fun, but it can also help you remember these important numbers.

TELEPHONE
Have you heard the latest gossip?

1. Players sit in a circle or a line. The more players you have, the sillier the game gets.

2. Choose one player to begin. That player makes up a short sentence and whispers it to the player to his left.

3. This player repeats what she heard, or what she thinks she heard, into the ear of the person to her left. Each player must listen carefully, because the sentence cannot be repeated.

4. The sentence continues around the circle until it reaches the player on the other side of the first player. She says the sentence she heard, and then the first player says what the original sentence was. The differences are often hilarious!

BACKWORDS
Tahw dnik fo emag si siht?

1. The first player chooses a short, easy-to-spell word.

2. He then says it out loud, but backward. This might be difficult for some people, so you can use a pencil and paper to figure it out. *Table* would be pronounced *"elbat."*

3. The other players take turns trying to figure out what the mystery word is. They might also need pencils and paper to figure it out. The first player should repeat the word as many times as necessary for the other players to figure it out.

4. The first player to figure out the mystery word chooses one of her own, and the game begins again.

For a longer game, use common phrases instead of words. Keep the words in their original order, or reverse them, too, for an even harder variation!

HINK PINKS
This name game is a fun one

1. One player thinks of a hink pink. A hink pink is made up of two one-syllable words that rhyme. For example, a pile of between-meal goodies is a "snack stack." Once the player has thought of a hink pink, she tells its definition to the other players. For example, thinking of a "mouse house," the first player tells the others, "A rodent's dwelling."

2. The other players take turns trying to guess the hink pink.

3. The first person to figure out the hink pink gets to make up her own, and the other players must guess what her hink pink is.

When you've run out of hink pinks, it's time to move on to "hinkie pinkies." A hinkie pinkie is like a hink pink, except it's made up of two two-syllable words. Here are some hinkie pinkies to get you started:

A tow-truck inspector—"wrecker checker"
A daisy's strength—"flower power"
A New York ball player who just struck out—"cranky Yankee"
A bigger battery—"larger charger"

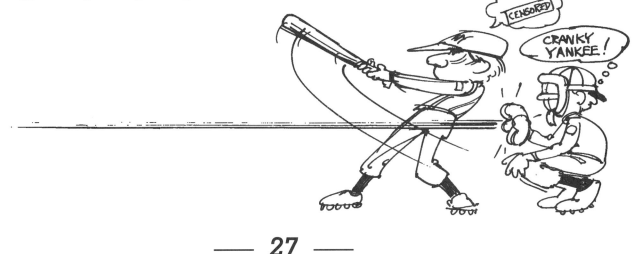

SUBSTITUTION FUN

Who can think up the funniest eyeball—er, phrase?

1. All the players agree on a key word that will be used in all the phrases. The weirder the key word, the funnier the game will be—try *eyeball, nostril,* or *rutabaga.*

2. Everyone takes turns substituting the key word for titles of songs, books, movies, or any other category you choose (or all these categories at once). *Eyeball* could be used in *Of Mice and Eyeballs; The Lion, the Witch, and the Eyeball;* or *The Hundred and One Eyeballs.*

3. The point of this game is to see who can come up with the funniest, weirdest title with your new word. Keep going until everyone is laughing, or until it seems like your key word isn't funny anymore. Pick a new one and start over.

ODD ONE OUT
Which thing doesn't belong?

1. The first player thinks of three different objects, with two of them sharing some quality and the third one lacking this same quality. A bird and an airplane share wings, for example, but a car doesn't. The differences can be in the objects themselves, or in the length or spelling of the words (*there* and *hair* rhyme with each other, for example, but *plant* doesn't rhyme with them). The quality can be as simple or as ridiculous as you want.

2. The first player tells the other players the three objects, and everyone takes turns trying to explain which one doesn't belong, and why.

3. The first player to figure out which object doesn't belong *and* correctly explain why is the winner. She chooses a new set of objects, and the game begins again.

Sometimes the reasons other people come up with for one object being different are better (or funnier, or stranger) than the first player's reasons. Vote on the best explanation, and the person with the most votes is the winner.

TABOO
Whatever you do, don't say it!

1. The first player tells everyone a letter of the alphabet that will be forbidden, or "taboo." She then asks the other players any question she likes.

2. Players take turns answering her question, using sensible phrases or sentences that do not contain the forbidden letter. The game should move quickly, with each player given only five seconds to come up with an answer.

3. If a player uses the taboo letter or gives an answer that doesn't make sense or doesn't answer the question, he is out.

4. When all players have had a turn, the first player asks a new question, keeping the same taboo letter. Play continues among the remaining players.

5. The last player remaining is the winner and chooses a new taboo letter and question for the next game.

MY AUNT SALLY IS STRANGE

How strange *is* she?

1. The first player begins by saying, "My aunt Sally is strange." Then he thinks of a rule for what Aunt Sally likes or doesn't like—for example, that she doesn't like words starting with s. Without actually saying the rule, he gives an example of it. In this case, he might say, "She likes fudge but hates sweets."

2. The other players then take turns guessing the rule that makes Aunt Sally strange. If all players have guessed once and haven't discovered the rule, the first player names another pair of things that, according to the rule, Aunt Sally likes and hates.

3. Play continues until someone discovers the rule, and then the game begins again with the winner thinking up a new rule.

4. The rules can be as normal or as strange as you can come up with—Aunt Sally only likes long green things, she only likes words containing e but not a, or she only likes things that can sweat. The weirder the rule, the longer and more hilarious the game becomes!

HOW GOOD IS YOUR MEMORY?

TRAVEL BINGO

The original and all-time favorite car game

This game requires advance preparation, but it's so easy you can prepare it on the road. Sometimes making the cards is almost as much fun as playing the game!

1. You will need to make up a different bingo card for each person, like the one shown at right. Make as many as you like, but have at least one for each person.

2. Fill in every square with things you think you'll see on the road. You can draw a small picture, or write the name of what you think you'll find. Examples include: a cow, a speed limit sign, a barn, a construction sign, a camper, and a cornfield.

BARN	4-WAY STOP	COW	HAY-STACK	CAT
GOAT	BILL-BOARD	SILO	GAS STATION	BUS
TRACTOR	PIG	FREE	CORN FIELD	BRIDGE
DETOUR SIGN	TOW-TRUCK	BIKER	CHICKEN	WATER TANK
FARMER	NEON SIGN	CAMPER	RIVER	TRAIN

3. One of the great things about Travel Bingo is that it can be used in cars, buses, or trains—even on a school bus trip—and you can adapt it to any part of the country. For a train ride through the Midwest in the fall, fill your card with tractors, silos, farmers, and barns. If you're driving through Maine in the winter, look for snowplows, trucks with chains, outdoor skating rinks, and ski slopes.

4. The middle square can be a FREE square for everyone, or you can fill it in with another item.

5. Once everyone has made a card, collect them all and mix them up, then hand them out again. Make sure that no players are using cards they made.

6. Now keep your eyes peeled for the things on your card. When you see one, tell everyone what you see, then mark it off on your card. You can mark on the cards with a felt-tip marker or crayon (make a small mark if you want to use the card again) or, for a train or smooth-driving car, find a flat surface and mark the squares by covering each one with a penny, button, or some other marker.

7. The first player to see five items in a row calls out "Bingo!" and is the winner. All the players clear the marks off their cards and the game begins again.

8. Keep a Travel Bingo set in your car or travel kit, with a good supply of buttons, pennies, or other markers. Make a new set of cards for each trip, but hold on to them when you're finished playing so you can use them again. You can build up a great collection of cards this way!

Bingo has many variations—play Four Corners (cover all four corners to win), the X Game (cover the two diagonal lines that meet in the center square), or Blackout (cover all the squares). Or make up shapes of your own! In all these games, the first player to cover the correct shape wins.

I SPY

I spy something with purple and green polka dots!

1. The first player begins by spotting something outside or inside the car, train, bus, or airplane. If the object is outside the vehicle, choose something that can be seen for a long time. Don't pick a billboard you're about to pass; choose a house in the distance.

2. The first player says, "I spy something . . ." and then tells what color the mystery object is.

3. Other players look inside and outside the vehicle, then take turns guessing the mystery object. The first player answers "Yes" or "No" to each guess.

4. The player who guesses the mystery object wins, then chooses another mystery object himself. The game also ends if the mystery object can't be seen anymore (for example, if you pass by something.) The first player then announces that the object can't be seen anymore and chooses a new mystery object.

A variation is Alphabet I Spy, where players take turns spotting objects in A-B-C order. The first player might say, "I spy an airplane," and the second player might say, "I spy a bicycle," and so on. The other players look for the object that has been spied and point it out when they find it. In another variation of this game, the first player has to spy something beginning with a and the other players have to look for the object, the second player has to spy something beginning with b, and so on through the alphabet.

VOWEL RACE
Find *AArdvArk* and score big

1. No more than five players can play this game. Each player chooses a vowel, or they can be randomly assigned.

2. Each player should have a sheet of paper and a marker or crayon to write down his score.

3. Whenever a player spots his vowel (on a road sign, billboard, or license plate), he calls out the word it appears in (or the license plate number), then marks his score on his paper.

4. If a vowel appears in more than one word on one object, or more than once in the same word, that player gets one point for every time the letter appears.

5. Once a player calls out a word or license plate, no other player may get points for her vowel in that same word or plate. For

example, if the player who has the vowel *i* says "miles," the e player does not get a point. But players who shout out the same word at the same time both get points for the word.

6. The first player to reach a certain score, or the highest score at your destination, wins. Note that players should decide beforehand whether to count mile markers (those small green signs on the sides of the highway), or any other frequently occurring sign that seems to favor one player or players over others.

A variation is to give bonus points for vowels appearing more than once in the same word or license plate. Give one point for the first appearance, two points for the second, and so on, rather than just one point for each appearance. *Believe* would then be worth six points to the e player (one point for the first e, two for the second, and three for the third), rather than just three (one for each e). You can do the same within a sign, giving bonus points for multiple vowel appearances. Be careful, though, because this can add up to a lot of points!

GUESSING GAMES
The only limit is your imagination!

1. One player (usually the driver) is chosen as the Quizmaster. She decides what is to be guessed and announces it: "Raise your hand when we've driven one mile" or "How many minutes until we see a yellow house?"

2. The Quizmaster can choose any question she wants, but it should relate to the trip and the surroundings. Try for questions that any player can answer, and that don't require looking on a map. Checking the odometer or looking at a map (or any other reference book) by any player other than the Quizmaster is not allowed.

3. Guessing Games can be played until one player reaches a certain number of correct answers, or until a certain number of questions have been asked, and the player with the most correct answers is the winner.

This game can easily be played in a car, bus, or train ("How long until the next town?" or "How many telephone poles will we pass in the next five minutes?") or an airplane ("What's the meal going to be today?" or "When will they start the in-flight movie?" or "How many exits are on the plane?"). Change Quizmasters when one person gets tired or runs out of questions.

I WENT TO THE STORE

Can you get all the way from A to Z?

1. In the classic version of this game, the first player begins by saying "I went to the store and bought . . ." and then names an item beginning with a that could be found at a store—apple, for example.

2. The next player says, "I went to the store and bought . . . ," then names what the first player bought, and adds an item beginning with b—bologna, for example.

3. Play continues with players taking turns adding an item to the list beginning with the next letter of the alphabet. The whole list must be recited each time.

4. If a player forgets an item, or can't think of one for his letter, he is out.

5. The last player remaining is the winner.

6. If more than one player remains when the alphabet has been completed, begin again, but this time all players must recite *both* lists (the completed A to Z list and the new items, too).

The alphabet list can be anything you like, from the difficult ("I bought a painting by . . .") to the bizarre ("My mother told me never to stick anything up my nose, especially not . . ."). Invent new and silly categories!

ALLITERATION ALPHABET

An alphabet memory game—times two

1. The first player begins by naming a two-word phrase with both of the words beginning with the letter a—"one amazing animal," for example. The two words must go together somehow. The first player can't say, "Apple Arizona," for example.

2. The next player must name the first player's item and add her own two-word phrase, with both words in her phrase beginning with b. She could say, for example, "One amazing animal, two beautiful bananas."

3. Play continues with the third player naming the other two items, then adding a third two-word phrase, with all words beginning with c, and so on through the alphabet.

4. If any player forgets an item or cannot name a new one when his turn comes around, he is out.

5. When only one player is left, she is the winner!

6. You might want to leave out Q, X, and Z, since these are hard letters to find words for.

7. If more than one player is left when the alphabet is completed, begin the game again among any remaining players. But this time, each player must name *three* words for each letter—"awfully angry ape," for example.

WHAT'S MISSING?

Try to remember the missing item— is it the rubber chicken?

1. The first player puts several different items in a paper bag. The more items in the bag, the harder the game.

2. The other players take turns looking in the bag, trying to memorize everything that's in it.

3. When all the players have looked in the bag, the first player secretly removes one object, then passes the bag back to the other players.

4. Each player then looks in the bag again and writes down on his own piece of paper which item he thinks is missing.

5. When all the players think they know the answer, the first player collects all the pieces of paper. The player with the correct answer is the winner.

6. In case of a tie, the game is played again among the players with the correct answers.

7. The winner then takes the bag from the first player, replaces the missing item, and removes another item, and the game begins again.

In case you don't have a bag, don't have enough items, or want the driver to play, too, the game can be played out loud. The first player reads a list of items three times while the other players listen. Then the first player reads out the list again in a different order, with one item missing. The first player to name the missing object is the winner.

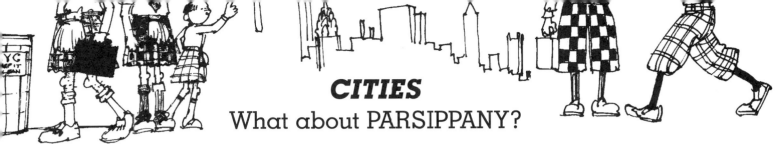

CITIES
What about PARSIPPANY?

1. One player names a city anywhere in the world. Longer city names make for a harder game.

2. The other players try to form sentences with the initial letters of the city. An answer for NEW YORK could be, "Not Everyone Wears Yellow Or Red Kilts."

3. The sentence should make grammatical sense, but it can be silly or outrageous.

4. After everyone has made up sentences, each player reads his out loud. Then everyone votes on the best sentence, and the player with the most votes wins.

5. The winner chooses a new city, and the game begins again.

A variation is to give a time limit—five minutes, for example. Only players who make a sentence in that amount of time stay in the game. The last player remaining wins. Or, using the time limit, give one point for every sentence made (no more than one sentence per player per city) and two points if the sentence actually says something real about the city. The first player to get ten points wins.

COW COUNTING

A game for when you're on the *moo*-ve

In the simplest form of this game, each player counts the cows on her side of the car. The first player to reach a predetermined number (such as fifty), or the player with the most cows when you arrive at your destination, wins.

Every family has its own variations of this game, and you can make up your own. Assign one point for each cow spotted and different points for other farm animals, for example. Pigs could be worth five points, goats ten points, and a white horse twenty-five points.

In other variations, passing a graveyard erases all your cows, and you start over at zero. You could take ten points off all players' scores for crossing over a railroad track, or add ten points to everyone's scores for passing under a railroad trestle.

PUNCH BUGGY
Count the Beetles!

In Punch Buggy, players earn points for spotting Volkswagen Beetles (or any other type of car). The first player to see a Beetle calls out, "Punch Buggy!" and the color of the car. Each Beetle is worth one point, and VW vans are worth ten. You can give different points for different colors of Beetles and vans. Be creative and flexible so everyone can have fun!

LICENSE PLATE GAMES

LICENSE PLATE ALPHABET

Who can get through the alphabet first?

1. The object of this game is to find every letter of the alphabet, in order, on license plates.

2. Each player watches license plates and calls out the letters as he sees them. Only the big letters on the license plates count, not the state name, motto, or any other words on or around the plate.

3. Letters must be called out in alphabetical order. Players may find more than one letter on a license plate.

4. The first player to call out "Z" is the winner.

On less crowded roads, players can work together to get through the alphabet, still finding the letters in order. The first player to find a letter calls it out, and she gets one point. When z is reached, the player with the most points wins.

LICENSE PLATE COUNTING
How high can you go?

1. Players begin this game by finding a plate with the number 1 on it.

2. The first player to find 1 shouts it out, and then looks for 2. Other players continue to look for a 1, and shout it out when they find it.

3. Counting continues, with players counting individually, until a certain number has been reached (like 30) or the car arrives at your destination. The first player to reach the target number, or the one with the highest number when you reach your destination, is the winner.

4. Each plate counts for only one player and only one number. Finding a plate with 123 might seem great, but it can count for only one number: 1, 2, 3, 12, or 23. Numbers 10 and higher must be found consecutively on the same plate, with no numbers in between (810 counts as 10, but 801 and 180 don't).

LICENSE PLATE MATH
Get to 59, but not any higher!

1. The first player begins with the first license plate that anyone sees. She adds the first and last number on the plate together, and then remembers (or writes down) that total.

2. The next player adds the first and last numbers of the second plate that anyone sees, and remembers his total.

3. Play continues with each player getting her own license plate, and adding the plate's first and last numbers to her total.

4. The first player to reach *exactly* 59 is the winner. If his total is more than 59, that player begins again at zero.

For extra addition practice, add up all the numbers in the license plate each time. Or, instead of adding the numbers together, simply place them together to make a two-digit number (5097 becomes 57, not 12). Try to bring the total to 500 (or some other large number).

LICENSE PLATE PHRASES

Every plate tells a story

1. All players agree to work from a particular license plate they see. The plate must contain at least three letters, and preferably more.

2. Each player tries to make up a phrase or sentence with the initials from the license plate in the same order. "NKN" could become "Nathan Knows Nothing."

3. When all players have made up phrases, everyone says hers. The funniest one wins.

You can also try to tell a story with consecutive license plates. Write down the phrases or sentences as you create them, so that you can keep track of your story. You can do this alone or in a group, with everyone voting on what the best sentence is.

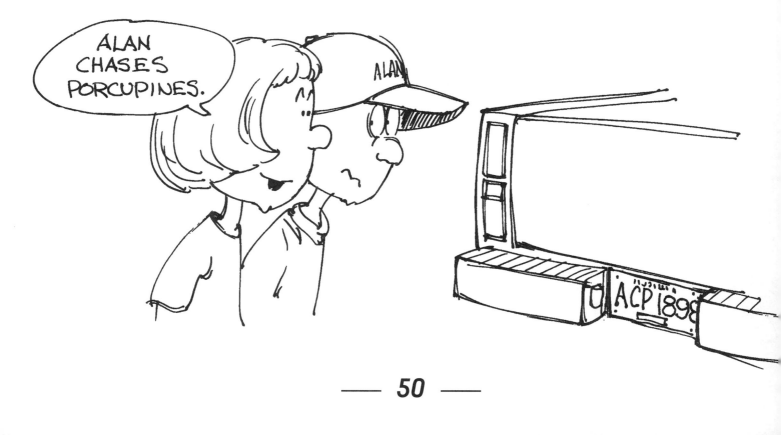

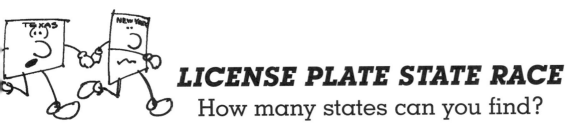

LICENSE PLATE STATE RACE
How many states can you find?

1. Each player tries to find a certain number of license plates from different states. Before the game begins, everyone should decide on how many need to be found. Ten or fifteen is a good range, but you can increase the number for long trips. Each player should get a marker and paper to write down the states she's found.

2. The first player to call out the state on a license plate marks that state on his paper. Other players may also find this state, but not from the same license plate.

3. The first player to reach the agreed number of states wins.

You can also play that once a state has been found, no other player may claim that state.

Another variation is to award points for each state, with more points for states that are farther away. (No points for your home state, one point for states bordering on your home state, two points for states that are one state away, and so on). This way, you can learn geography, too!

Or you can collect state mottoes or designs instead of states. Some states have plates with different designs—supporting the environment or education, for example, or declaring that the driver is a teacher or war veteran, or that the car is an antique. Other states have changed their license plate mottoes over the years, so you might find license plates from one state with more than one motto. Count each motto or design separately.

LICENSE PLATE WORDS
Wht wrd is hre?

1. Begin by choosing a license plate that has at least three letters but doesn't already contain a word. Everyone should write down all the letters.

2. Each player tries to make a word containing all of the letters in the license plate, in the order they appear there. Other letters may be inserted between the letters, but they must remain in the same order. *RLD* could be *rolled,* for example, but not *drill.*

3. The first player to create a word shouts it out and is the winner. Choose a new license plate and begin the game again.

You can also try to come up with the longest word containing the license plate's letters. Or you can count only words that contain the letters in the proper order, without any other letters in between them.

TWENTY-ONE
The more numbers the better

1. In this game, players add up all the single digits they see on license plates. "5JKL89" would add up to 22 (5+8+9).

2. Players look for license plates whose numbers add up to twenty-one or more. Note that license plates with three numbers or more are the only ones that will work for this game. If you are in a state with fewer than three numbers, multiply the two numbers on a plate to see if the product is higher than twenty-one.

3. When a player sees a plate whose total is higher than twenty-one, she calls it out and earns a point. Players calling out the same plate at the same time both earn a point.

4. The first player to get ten points wins.

STATES AND MOTTOES

"Oklahoma is OK!" but what's Tennessee?

1. Each player should make two columns on a sheet of paper. Label one column "States" and the other "Mottoes." Write the names of all fifty states, plus Washington, D.C., down the side of the "States" column.

2. The object is to find as many states and mottoes as you can. When a player spots a new plate, he calls it out, then marks an *X* next to that state on his list. If the plate also has a motto, he writes it in the "motto" column.

3. Players earn one point for each state and two points for each motto. Even if a player has already marked down a state, she may continue to look for a plate from that state that also contains the motto in order to get points for both.

4. The first player to get twenty-five points, or the person with the highest score at the end of the trip, is the winner.

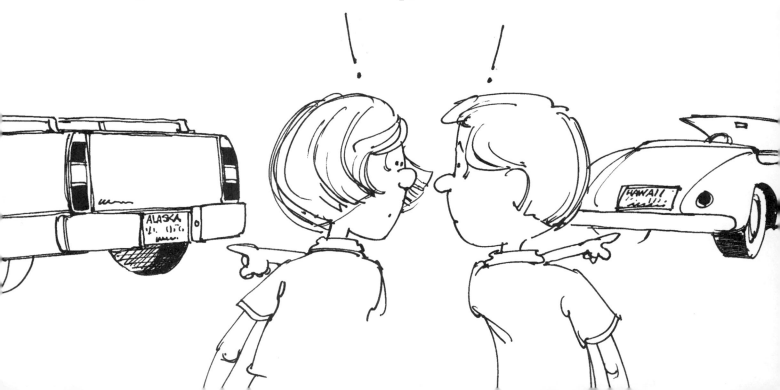

WRITING GAMES

HANGMAN
Guess the mystery word or be hanged!

Number of players: Two or more

1. Choose one player to be the Hangman. The Hangman then thinks up a mystery word for the other players to guess.

2. On a blank sheet of paper, the Hangman writes one dash for each letter of the mystery word. For example, the word *garbage* would have seven dashes.

3. The other players take turns guessing letters in the mystery word. If the letter is in the word, the Hangman writes it above the appropriate dash or dashes.

4. If the guess is wrong, the Hangman draws the base of the gallows. For each wrong guess that follows, the Hangman adds another part to the gallows. Once the gallows is finished, each wrong guess adds one body part hanging from the gallows, beginning with the head. The complete figure looks like the one above.

5. The Hangman keeps track of wrong guesses by writing those letters next to the gallows.

6. If a player guesses the word before the Hangman finishes drawing a body on the gallows, that player wins!

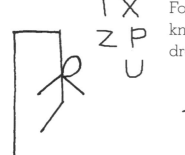

For a more difficult game, choose a mystery phrase or well-known saying. You can also make the game last longer by drawing more body parts—a face, hands, or feet.

G _ _ R _ _ G _

MEDITERRANEAN

Find as many words as fish in the sea

Number of players: Two or more

1. All players agree on a long word to use, like *Mediterranean* or *antidisestablishmentarianism*. Each player writes the long word at the top of a piece of paper.

2. Each player tries to form as many words as possible, using only the letters in the long word. If a letter appears only once in the long word, it can appear only once in any of your shorter words. Letters can be used again in different words.

3. Players keep working until everyone's finished, or until a set time (ten minutes, for instance) has passed. The player with the longest list wins.

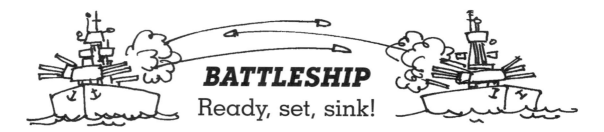

BATTLESHIP
Ready, set, sink!

Number of players: Two

1. Each player draws two separate grids of ten rows and ten columns on a blank piece of paper. That way each player has two large squares, each containing one hundred smaller squares. Graph paper is best for this game.

2. Mark the rows on each grid with the numbers one through ten and the columns with the letters *A* through *J*. Each player marks the left grid *Ships* and the right grid *Shots*.

3. Without letting his opponent see, each player places five "ships," either horizontally or vertically, on the Ships grid. This is done by shading the correct number of squares in a row for each ship and writing the name of the ship near the squares it occupies. Each player has an aircraft carrier (which fills five spaces), a battleship (five spaces), a cruiser (four spaces), a destroyer (three spaces), and a submarine (two spaces).

4. When both players have placed all their ships, the first player begins by calling out a square where he thinks his opponent's ships might be. Grid squares are named with the letter and number that correspond to the column and row the square occupies (A-8, C-10, or F-1, for example).

5. If the player calls out a square on which one of his opponent's ships is located, the second player says "Hit!" and tells him which ship he has hit. Otherwise, the second player says "Miss."

6. The second player then takes her turn, calling out a square she thinks might be part of one of her opponent's ships. No extra turn is earned for a hit.

7. Each player keeps track of his own guesses on the Shots grid, marking each hit with an *X*. Misses are marked down with a dot, so that the same square is not called out twice.

8. Once a player has hit all the squares occupied by a ship, he has sunk that ship. The first player to sink all of her opponent's ships is the winner.

Hint: If a player scores a hit, she should make her next guess in one of the squares next to the one she hit. This will tell her whether the ship has been placed horizontally or vertically, and therefore where her next guesses should be.

For a longer game, make a larger grid and add more ships.

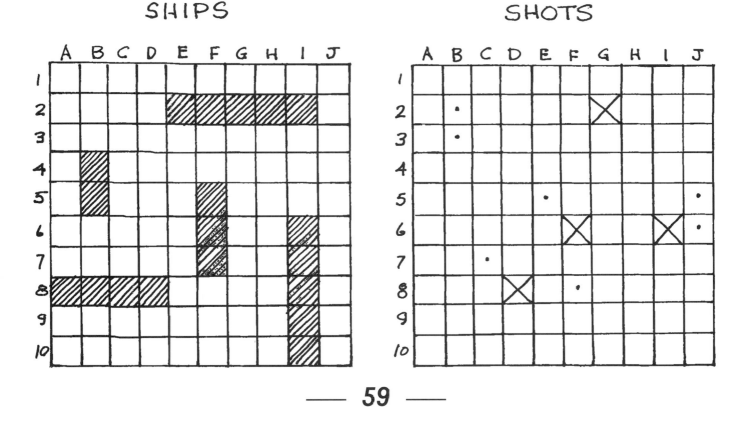

BATTLE OF TRAFALGAR
The Official Game of the French Naval Academy

Number of players: Two

1. The basic setup of this game is the same as Battleship (see page 58), but the rules are more complicated. Draw two grids and place your ships as in steps 1 through 3 of Battleship. Because the boats can move, you may need to use more than one Ships grid for each game, or draw your ships in lightly. Rather than shading squares in, you might find it easier to mark the squares your aircraft carrier is in with *A*'s, your destroyers with *D*'s, and so forth.

2. In the Battle of Trafalgar, ships can shoot or move, but cannot do both in one turn. Submarines can move three squares or shoot once in a turn, cruisers and destroyers can move two squares or shoot twice, and battleships and aircraft carriers can move one square or shoot three times.

SHIPS

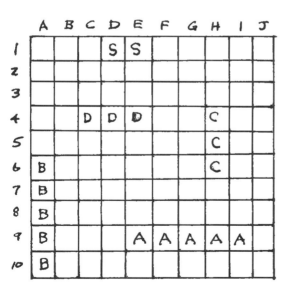

SHOTS

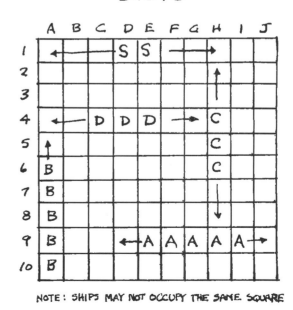

NOTE: SHIPS MAY NOT OCCUPY THE SAME SQUARE

3. In her turn, a player calls out no more than three shots, or says that she is moving. She calls out her shots as in Battleship but does not need to say which ships are shooting.

4. If the first player has shot, the other player tells which ship was hit and which square the hit fell into.

5. The first player should mark her shots separately from her hits, since a ship may move into a square that was previously a miss. She marks any hits on the Shots diagram and lists any misses to the side. It's a good idea to keep track of which turn a shot was made in the list of misses.

6. The second player then takes his turn, moving or calling out his shots.

7. A player may move only one ship per turn, although his shots can come from several ships.

8. In moving ships, he can move only forward or backward—not sideways or diagonally. Players may turn their ships to face a different direction, but that move takes up a whole turn (regardless of what kind of ship is being moved).

9. A ship that is hit can continue to shoot until it is sunk, but it can no longer move.

10. The game ends when one player loses all his ships, or when both players have only ships that are unable to move. If ships are remaining, the player who suffered the fewest hits is the winner.

For a simpler and shorter game, place only three ships at the beginning of the game.

TIC-TAC-TOE

A classic pencil game, with some new twists

Number of players: Two

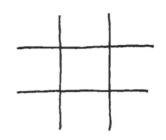

1. To play regular Tic-Tac-Toe, draw the game board on a blank piece of paper.

2. The first player writes an *X* in one of the game spaces, and the second player follows by writing an *O* in another space.

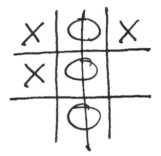

3. The two players take turns making their marks, and the first one to get three in a row (up, down, or from corner to corner) is the winner. In case of a tie, in which neither player gets three in a row, play again.

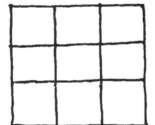

TIC-TAC-TOE SQUARED

1. Draw the same game board as in Tic-Tac-Toe, but draw a square around the whole board to make nine boxes.

2. Players take turns as in Tic-Tac-Toe, but they make their marks where the lines cross, rather than in the spaces in between the lines. The outside lines are included in the game board so that there are sixteen places to make a mark.

3. Even though it is possible to make four marks in a row, the winner is still the first player to get three consecutive marks.

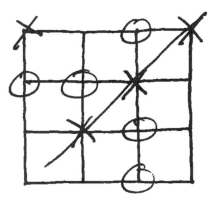

TIC-TAC-TOE-TOE
1. Add another row and column of boxes to the Tic-Tac-Toe Squared board so that there are sixteen boxes in all.

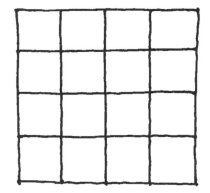

2. As in Tic-Tac-Toe Squared, the players make their marks at the intersections of lines and not in the spaces in between the lines.

3. To win Tic-Tac-Toe-Toe, however, a player must get *four* consecutive marks, although it is possible to make five marks in a row on the game board.

For a longer, more challenging game, make an even bigger board and try to get five marks in a row!

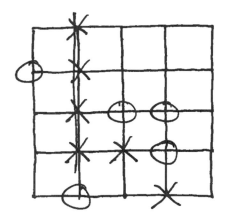

EXQUISITE CORPSE
It's not as gross as it sounds!

Number of players: Two or more

1. Take a piece of paper and fold it, top to bottom, into thirds. Keep it folded so that only one section is visible at a time.

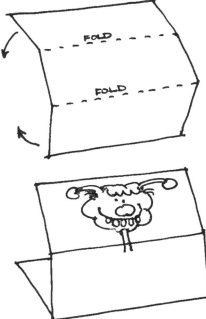

2. The first player draws a head for Exquisite Corpse, then folds the paper over so that just the section below it is visible and his section cannot be seen. (It's a good idea to extend the neck of the Corpse slightly below the first section so the next person knows where to attach the body.)

3. The next person draws the body and arms (not the legs) of the Corpse, again extending it slightly into the next section. She folds the paper so that the third section is visible, and passes it along to the next player.

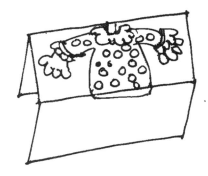

4. The third player adds the legs and feet (perhaps a tail, too) of the corpse, then unfolds the paper so that everyone can see what's been created.

You can adapt this game for different numbers of players. Two players can take turns drawing. More players can add sections to the Corpse, with one person drawing the top of the head, the next person the bottom half, the third person the neck and shoulders, and so forth.

Or, instead of drawing, you can make an Exquisite Corpse story. Fold a piece of paper as in step 1, then write the beginning of a story, writing only one sentence on the next section. The next player must continue the story, building on the sentence he is given. Then he passes the paper along to the next person, and so forth. You can make the story as long (or short) as you want, depending on how many players you have, or how long you want to keep writing. Just fold the paper into more sections.

TAXICAB
How many passengers can you deliver?

Number of players: One or more

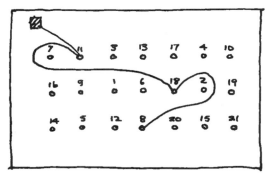

1. Each player needs to draw a diagram with three rows of seven dots, numbered from one to twenty-one in no particular order. They must be numbered differently for each player, and no two numbers can be consecutive. The square at the top left of the paper is the garage.

2. Players take turns giving each other taxi rides. The first player calls out a number to another player. That player draws a line from his garage to the numbered dot on his page.

3. The player who picked up the passenger then calls out another number to another player, and so forth. Players should not look at each other's diagrams.

4. The first ride always begins at the garage, but every ride after that begins at the numbered dot where the player picked up his last passenger. No dot may be used twice by the same player, so if a fare (numbered dot) is called out to that player and she has already used that numbered dot, the player calling out the fare must choose another one.

5. At no time during the game can any lines on a player's diagram cross. If he cannot visit a number because it is surrounded by lines, he is out of the game.

6. The game continues until all players have been eliminated. Everyone counts up the number of fares (numbered dots) each player picked up. The person with the most fares wins.

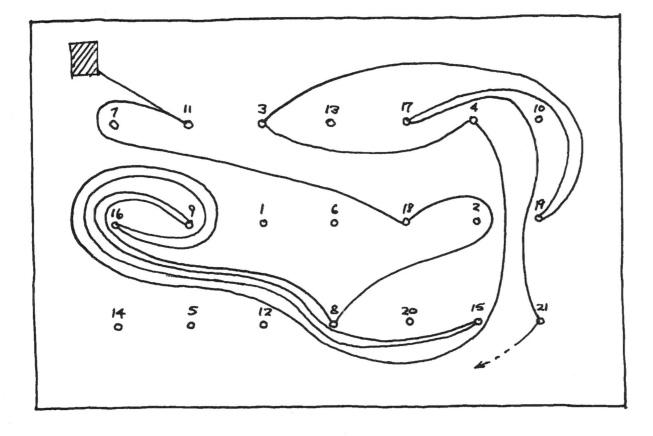

By picking numbers from a hat, one person can play this game.

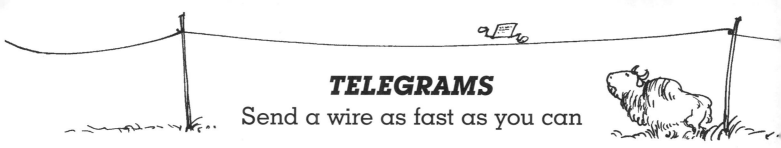

TELEGRAMS
Send a wire as fast as you can

Number of players: Two or more

Before telephones were invented, the fastest way to communicate was by telegram, in which a message was coded letter by letter and sent over a wire to another station, where the message was decoded. Telegraph companies charged per word, so telegrams often left out unimportant words.

1. Each player needs a pencil and a piece of paper. In turn, each player names a letter until there are at least five letters (some letters may be repeated). Or, you can choose letters out of a hat.

2. All players write the letters, in the order they are given, at the top of their papers.

3. Everyone tries to form a telegram whose initials are the given letters. For example, if the letters are SIPEBT, a telegram might be "Swimming In Portland. Eating Big Tacos." The telegram needs to make sense, although telegrams often drop certain shorter or unimportant words from a sentence.

4. The first player to come up with a telegram reads it out. He is the winner. Pick a new set of letters and play again!

You can also require the telegrams to be about a certain subject, from a certain location, or to a certain person. Or, instead of having the fastest telegram as the winner, have everyone vote on the funniest or best telegram. The person with the most votes wins.

DOTS

Connect the dots to make the most squares and win!

Number of players: Two or more

1. To make the playing board, draw a grid with an equal number of rows and columns of dots. Ten rows and ten columns is a good size to start.

2. Each player takes turns drawing a line between two dots that are next to each other. The lines may go in any direction except diagonally.

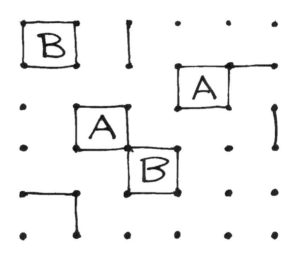

3. Whenever a player draws a line that completes a square, she writes her first initial in the middle of the square and takes another turn.

4. If she is able to, the player can use this extra turn to complete another square. With proper planning, a player can make lots of squares in a row, especially late in the game.

5. When the board is filled, players count up the number of squares they made. The one with the most squares wins!

SQUIGGLES
Make it pretty or silly

Number of players: Two or more

1. The first player draws a squiggly line on a blank piece of paper.

2. The next player must draw a picture, using this line as some part of the drawing.

3. When the player finishes her picture, she makes a squiggle on a new piece of paper and passes it along to the next player, who turns the new squiggle into another picture.

Be as creative as possible! You can even combine several squiggle drawings together to make a scene.

GEOGRAPHY GAMES

MAGELLAN
Who can find the shortest route?

1. For this game, you'll need at least one map with distances marked on it. It's best to have multiple copies of the same map, but if necessary players can trade one map back and forth.

2. Two cities to travel between are chosen, the farther apart the better. They can be the beginning and ending destinations of your trip, or any two cities you like, such as Chicago and Los Angeles.

3. Players then try to find the shortest route between the two cities, using the distances marked on the map. Routes can travel along any roads you like, from four-lane interstates to tiny county roads.

4. When the first player finds a route, he adds up the distances along it and announces the total. The next player then tries to find a shorter route. The game continues until one player has found the shortest possible route.

You can also permit travel only along major interstates, or only along smaller roads, such as state roads or county roads. Or you can require routes to travel through certain states or cities, or give bonus points (reduced mileage) for the fewest states traveled through, or make up your own bonuses and penalties.

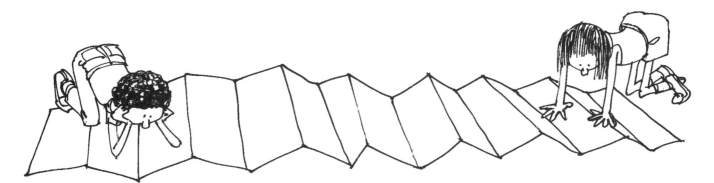

ACRONYM ROUTES
Will you go to RENO or POUGHKEEPSIE?

1. This game can be played with or without a map, but it's much easier to play with one. Either way, both players will need paper and a marker or crayon.

2. The first player begins by selecting a starting city and a destination city. She tries to find a route from one city to the other, traveling through cities that spell the second city's name. For example, an acronym route from Birmingham, Alabama, to MEMPHIS, Tennessee, might go through Manchester, Alabama; Eldridge, Alabama; Mantatchie, Mississippi; Plantersville, Mississippi; Hickory Flat, Mississippi; Independence, Mississippi; and Southaven, Mississippi.

3. The cities along the route must appear in order (no backtracking allowed) from one city to the next. Zigzagging back and forth along a main road is permitted, as long as each stop takes you closer to the destination.

4. The shortest route need not be taken. In fact, for longer names, or for games played without a map, you might find an acronym route that goes between two fairly close cities by traveling the *other* way around the world to get there.

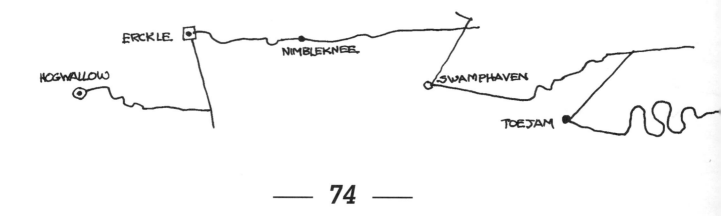

5. Once the first player has found an acronym route, she announces that she has found one to the second player, who now must figure out an acronym route between the two cities. It does not have to be the same route taken as the first player, as long as it follows the rules of the game.

6. When he has found an acronym route, he shows it to the first player, then chooses a new one for the first player to figure out.

7. A winner can be chosen in a variety of ways. Players can time each other, and the fastest to discover a route (or a series of routes) is the winner. Or the distance of the acronym route can be measured, and the shortest (or longest) route is the winner. Or you can just keep passing the map back and forth, challenging each other with longer and longer city names, until one player is finally stumped.

You can vary the game by requiring all routes to stay within the same hemisphere, continent, country, or state, or by assigning a bonus point system, with extra points for routes that travel (or don't travel) over oceans, rivers, county lines, or country borders, or that stay on major highways. The highest-scoring route is the winner.

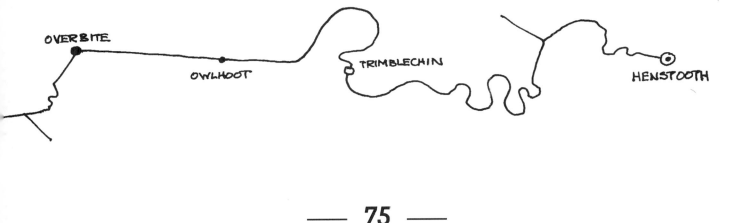

MAP DETECTIVE
Is it the smallest name—or the biggest?

1. For this game, you'll need a map or an atlas. It can be of the region you're traveling in, or any region, and this game can be played with old maps or new ones. This is a game best suited to just two players. If more want to play, they need to be sitting next to one another, or have copies of the same maps.

2. One player finds a name on the map or on a page of the atlas, and then passes the map to the other player (or players). The name can be of a region, river, town, mountain range—any name that appears on the map.

3. The other players try to find that name. The first player to find it is the winner, and finds a name of her own.

4. If there are only two players, players take turns searching for the names that each has chosen. You can time each other, with the winner being the player who has the fastest total time for five searches.

5. Most of the time, players look for the smallest name on the map, but sometimes the largest names are harder to find, since everyone starts concentrating on all the little names and doesn't notice the huge letters scattered across the map. So hide and seek wisely!

GEOGRAPHY
The fastest way to get from Japan to Nevada

1. The first player begins the game by giving the name of a geographical location, either a city, state, country, body of water, mountain, or island. Players can decide at the beginning of the game whether to allow all of these categories or only certain ones—for example, just the names of cities.

2. The next player must say another place whose name begins with the *last* letter of the word given by the first player. For example, if the first player says "Mississippi," then the second player could say "Indiana," the third player could say "Arkansas," and so on.

3. If a player repeats another player's word, or cannot give a word within a fair amount of time, she is out. The game continues with the next player. The last player to remain in is the winner!

Geography can be played with other categories, too, such as the names of famous people or fictional characters, movie or book titles, or whatever else you and your friends find interesting.

GEOGRAPHY BRAINTEASERS

In what state is your mind?

STATE OF CONFUSION!

Here's a fun way to test your knowledge about the United States. Answers on page 111.

1. Name all the states in the United States that end with the letter a.

2. Which states are spelled with letters that appear only once?

3. Which states are spelled using only four different letters? (Hint: Their names may be longer than four letters.)

4. Which states have the following nicknames?

    a. Golden State

    b. Sunshine State

    c. Ocean State

    d. Aloha State

e. First State

f. Show Me State

g. Silver State

h. The Last Frontier

i. Bluegrass State

j. Grand Canyon State

k. Bay State

l. Land of Enchantment

m. Heart of Dixie

5. Which states border the Atlantic Ocean?

6. Which states border the Pacific Ocean?

STATE FLASH CARDS
A flashy way to learn your state facts

1. This game requires advance preparation, although some of it can be done on the trip. You'll need tracing paper, as well as fifty index cards or pieces of poster board.

2. Before the trip, use the tracing paper to trace the shape of each state from a map of the United States. Cut out each state shape and trace it onto fifty index cards or pieces of poster board. Then once again cut out each state shape. For Hawaii, you can just trace around the largest island (Hawaii), and you don't need to draw the smaller islands that are part of Alaska.

3. On the reverse of each state shape, write the state's name, as well as the state capital. Because Colorado and Wyoming are both rectangles of similar size, place a dot on each one where the state capital is so that you can learn to tell them apart.

4. When you're ready to play, divide up the cards evenly among all the players. Players take turns holding up state shapes, and the first player to recognize the state calls it out and wins that shape. He collects that card and places it to the side. Then he holds up one of his shapes (but not any that he has won).

5. The game continues until all the players have shown all of their state shapes. When one player wins a card but has run out of shapes, the player on her right continues the game by holding up a card.

6. When all cards have been won, the player with the most cards wins.

As players become familiar with state shapes, you can require them to also name the state capital to win the card. If a player is the first to name a state but cannot name the capital, the card is returned to the player who showed it. That player returns the card to his pile to show later, and continues the game by showing another card.

When everyone has learned the states and capitals, include more information about the state, such as major rivers, other major cities, state parks, or neighboring states. When a player identifies the state and its capital, she may then earn bonus points by naming as many of these facts about the state as she can. Each correct answer earns one point. At the end of the game, total all cards won (counting each as one point), and all bonus questions correctly answered. The player with the most points is the winner.

JOKES AND RIDDLES

BRAINTEASERS

Now it's time to give your mind a real workout!

One day two fathers and two sons went fishing. At the end of the day, each had caught one fish, but there were only three fish in all. How can this be true?

A grandfather, his son, and his grandson were the ones who went fishing.

Sara Jones has the same number of brothers as sisters, but her brother Sam has twice as many sisters as he has brothers. How many children in the Jones family?

Seven—four daughters and three sons.

How long would it take you to cut a log into ten pieces if each cut takes one minute?

Nine minutes—ten pieces take only nine cuts.

What is the next letter in the following sequence—JFMAMJ?

J—they're the first letter of the months of the year, January through June.

How do you give someone $63 using six bills, none of which are $1 bills?

One $50, one $5, and four $2 bills.

Mike bragged about his softball team, "Three of our men hit home runs, and two of those were grand slams. We won 9 to 0, but not a single man crossed the plate." How is this possible?

All of the players were married.

Two soldiers stood at attention, one facing north and the other facing south. One of the soldiers asked the other, "Why are you smiling?" How did he know the other soldier was smiling?

The soldiers were facing each other.

Jack planned to get to work ten minutes early. He thought his watch was ten minutes slow, but actually it was fifteen minutes fast. Was Jack early, late, or on time for work?

Jack was thirty-five minutes early. (Add the ten minutes he planned to arrive early plus the ten minutes he believed his watch was slow plus the fifteen minutes his watch was fast.)

A used car dealer sold sixty cars during a six-day period. Each day he sold four more cars than he did the day before. How many cars did he sell on the first day?

None. (On the first day, he sold none; on the second day, four; on the third, eight; on the fourth, twelve; on the fifth, sixteen; and on the sixth, twenty.)

— *84* —

A train one mile long is traveling at a speed of one mile per minute through a tunnel one mile long. How long will it take the train to pass completely through the tunnel?

Two minutes.

Brett is eating at Tom's Diner and finds a fly in his coffee, then calls the waiter over to get a fresh cup. When the waiter returns, Brett takes just one sip and says, "This is the same cup I had before!" How did he know?

He'd put sugar in the coffee before finding the fly.

Susie and Sara were born on the same day of the same year from the same mother and father, but they are not twins. How can this be possible?

Susie and Sara are two out of a set of triplets.

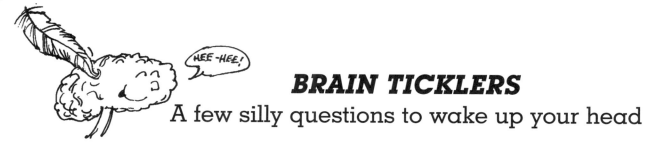

BRAIN TICKLERS
A few silly questions to wake up your head

If one man carries a sack of flour and another man carries two sacks, who has the heavier load?

The one with a sack of flour, which is heavier than just two empty sacks.

What starts with a _T_, ends with a _T_, and is full of _T_?

A teapot.

Two turtles tied twine to a tree to trick Tommy Tucker into a trap. How many _T_'s are there in that?

There are only two _T_'s in that.

What three-syllable word contains all twenty-six letters?

Alphabet.

What does a dog have that nothing else can?

Puppies.

What has cities with no houses, rivers without water, and forests without trees?

A map.

What flies when it's on and floats when it's off?

A feather.

What has a big mouth but can't talk?

A jar.

What question can you never answer "Yes" to?

"Are you asleep?"

With what vegetable do you throw away the outside, cook the inside, eat the outside, then throw away the inside?

Corn on the cob.

Would you rather an elephant attacked you or a gorilla?

You'd probably prefer it the elephant attacked the gorilla.

What kind of cup doesn't hold water?

A cupcake.

What does Germany produce that no other country does?

Germans.

What two things *can't* you have for breakfast?

Lunch and dinner.

Why won't basketball players be wearing their pants any longer?

They're long enough already.

What ten letter word starts with g-a-s?

Automobile.

What doesn't ask a question but needs to be answered?

The telephone and the doorbell.

Why does a mother carry her baby?

Because the baby can't carry the mother.

FASTER, MOM! FASTER!

What is a lamb after it is six months old?

Seven months old.

A dog is tied to a fifteen-foot rope but still manages to walk one hundred feet. How?

The rope wasn't tied to anything.

What did the dog say after he ate his dinner?

Nothing, silly. Dogs can't talk.

URP!

Which will burn longer—twelve candles on a cake or ten candles on a cake?

Neither—candles burn shorter, not longer.

A man makes more than a million dollars every day, but he isn't rich. Why not?

He works at the mint.

A police officer sees a school bus driver going the wrong way down a one-way street, but he doesn't stop the driver. Why not?

The bus driver was walking.

Before Mount Everest was discovered, what was the tallest mountain in the world?

Mount Everest.

How many three-cent stamps are in a dozen?

Twelve.

Forward I'm heavy, backward I'm not. What am I?

The word ton.

What five-letter word does every Harvard graduate pronounce wrong?

The word wrong.

What can speak any language in the world?

An echo.

What's the difference between an old dime and a new nickel?

Five cents.

What runs around town all day and lies on the floor at night with its tongue hanging out?

Your shoe.

What do you break by naming it?

Silence.

Why are people so tired on April 1?

They've just finished a March of thirty-one days.

Which is bigger, Mrs. Bigger or Mrs. Bigger's baby?

The baby's just a little Bigger.

What should you know before trying to teach tricks to a dog?

More than the dog.

A squirrel finds six ears of corn in a stump. How many trips will it take him to take all the corn away, if he can carry only three ears out of the stump each time?

Six, because he's got to carry his own two ears out each time.

If a man and a goose were in a runaway balloon and the man had no parachute, how could he get down?

He could get down by plucking the goose.

POEM RIDDLES
There's some reason behind these rhymes

I go but never stir,
I count but never write,
I measure and divide, sir,
You'll find my measures right.
I run but never walk,
I strike but never wound,
I tell you much but never talk
In all my daily round.

A clock.

Three-fourths of me an act display,
Three-fourths a bed for man.
Three-fourths have legs that cannot stray,
Three-fourths have legs that can.
I have a back without a spine,
An arm without a bone is mine.

The word coat. Three of its four letters spell act, cot (a bed with legs that "cannot stray"), and cat (which has legs and can stray).

Pray tell me, ladies, if you can,
Who is that much-loved man,
Who, though he has married many a wife,
May still live single all his life?

A priest.

The beginning of eternity,
The end of time and space,
The beginning of every end,
The end of every place.

The letter e.

I stop at every home that you may meet,
As I daily make my way along each street.
Take one letter from me and still you'll see
I'm the same as before, as I always will be;
Take two letters from me, or three or four,
I'll still be the same as I was before.
In fact, I'll say that all my letters you may take,
Yet of me nothing else you'll make.

A mail carrier.

Just equal are my head and tail,
My middle slender as can be,
Whether I stand on head or heel,
'Tis all the same to you or me.
But if my head should be cut off,
The matter's true, although 'tis strange,
My head and body, severed thus,
Immediately to nothing change.

The number 8.

Light as a feather, there's nothing in it;
But the strongest man can't hold it for more than a minute.

Breath.

What can run but never walks,
Has a mouth but never talks,
Has a head but never weeps,
Has a bed but never sleeps?

A river.

There is a thing that nothing is,
And yet it has a name.
It's sometimes tall and sometimes short,
Joins our talks and joins our sports,
And plays at every game.

A shadow.

Pronounced as one letter,
And written with three,
Two letters there are,
And two only in me.
I'm double, I'm single,
I'm black, blue, and gray,
I'm read from both ends
And the same either way.

Eye.

I THINK I'M BEING FOLLOWED!

There are three of us in two,
Five of us in seven,
Four of us in nine
And six in eleven.

Letters.

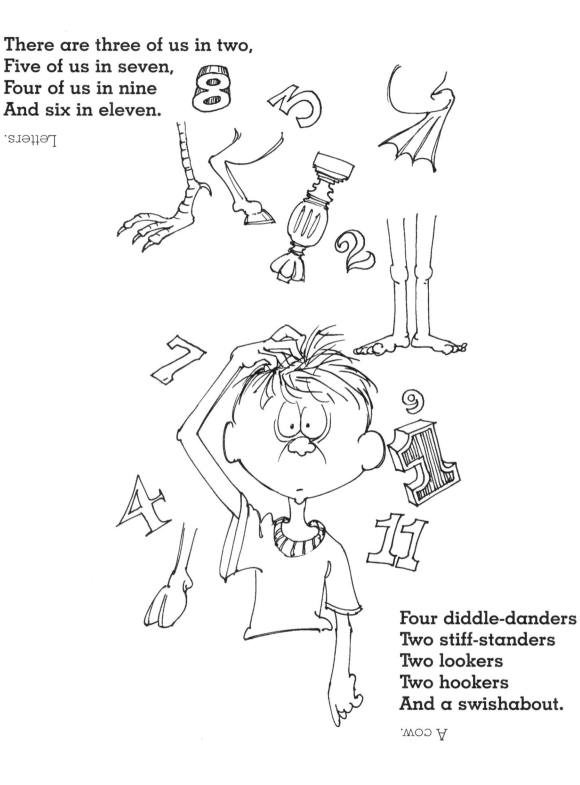

Four diddle-danders
Two stiff-standers
Two lookers
Two hookers
And a swishabout.

A cow.

I've seen you where you never were
And where you ne'er will be;
And yet you in that very same place
May still be seen by me.

Your face in a mirror.

Thirty white horses
Upon a red hill,
Now they tramp,
Now they champ,
Now they stand still.

Teeth and gums.

What's in the church
But not the steeple?
The parson has it,
But not the people.

The letter r.

SILLY STORIES
When you finally get to the end, you'll wish you hadn't!

In an effort to bring in money for renovations, a monastery decides to open a restaurant and serve fish and chips. Business is booming, so a local food critic decides to pay the monastery a visit. When his food is served, the fish is so underdone that he decides to complain to the cook in person. He marches back to the kitchen and grabs the first person in a robe he sees. "Are you the fish friar?" the food critic demands.

"Nope," says the brother he grabbed. "I'm the chip monk."

Two men are fishing for carp in a lake. When one catches a fish, the other man leans over the side of the boat to net his catch. In doing so, his wallet falls into the water and begins to sink to the bottom. He helplessly watches the wallet sink, until a fish suddenly swims underneath it and spits the wallet up in the air, over the boat, and to a fish on the other side! The other fish catches the wallet in his mouth, then spits it back to the first fish. The second man watches this game of catch in amazement, and his friend remarks, "You know, that's the first time I've ever seen real carp-to-carp walleting."

Three animals sat in a forest, arguing over who was the most powerful animal of all. The hawk claimed that he could fly from any danger and attack his prey from the air, where few animals expected it. The lion explained that his legendary strength and courage spoke for themselves. The skunk said that no animal would dare attack him, because of how he could make them smell. While the animals were arguing, a grizzly bear wandered past and took them all by surprise, swallowing them hawk, lion, and stinker.

In an effort to be kinder to animals, a new king declared that no more wild animals could be killed in his country. This policy worked for several years, but the population of lions, tigers, and other animals soon grew too large, and they began roaming the streets, hungry and looking for people to eat. The king's subjects soon rebelled against this new policy and removed him from power. This was perhaps the first time a reign was called on account of game.

An elephant and a giraffe were drinking at a river, when the elephant looked up at a turtle swimming nearby. Without a moment's hesitation, he suddenly ran over, picked up the turtle, and threw him hundreds of yards away. Satisfied, he returned to drink next to the giraffe.

"What did you do that for?" the giraffe asked the elephant.

"About forty years ago, that turtle bit my trunk when I was taking a drink," the elephant replied.

"So it's true what they say about you elephants," the giraffe marveled. "You never do forget."

"That's right," said the elephant. "Turtle recall."

The ruler of a small country commissioned his royal carvers to make him a new mahogany throne to replace his old one. Months later, having finished it, they wanted to sell off the king's old throne to pay for their costs in making the new one.

"Never," the king said. "It has too much sentimental value to me." And so the king stored the throne in the attic of his royal hut. Unfortunately, his hut (like those of his people) was made of grass, and the ceiling couldn't bear the weight of the old throne. The whole royal hut collapsed on itself.

When the king asked his advisers what he had done wrong, their answer was simple. "People in grass houses," they told him, "shouldn't stow thrones."

When Leif Eriksson came back from Greenland after a long voyage, he found that the most recent census of Norse citizens hadn't included him. Enraged that he had been forgotten while he was gone, he went to complain to the census taker, a small, nervous man. After Eriksson explained the problem, the census taker shook with fright and apologized. "I don't know what happened," he explained. "I must have taken Leif off my census."

Mr. and Mrs. Potato welcomed their daughter home from college one Christmas. Little Ann Potato was bursting with news for her parents.

"I've met a man," she told them. "And we're going to be married."

"How wonderful!" said Mrs. Potato. "Who is this lucky man?"

"Well," Ann told her parents, "you've probably heard of him. It's Dan Rather, the newsman."

Looks of concern crossed the faces of Mr. and Mrs. Potato. "I don't know about this marriage," said Mr. Potato. "It doesn't seem right to me."

"Why not?" asked Ann. "He's famous and wealthy, so he'll take good care of me—and, most importantly, we love each other."

"Dear, dear," said Mrs. Potato. "That sounds all well and good, but you need to understand—you're our precious little Ann Potato, the light of our life, and we want only the best for you. And Dan Rather—well, he's just a common tater."

PUNNY PLACES

Here's a punny conversation that's a geography lesson, too

Waiter:	Hawaii doing today? Are you Hungary?
Customer:	Yes, Siam. But I'm in a hurry and can't Romania long. Venice lunch going to be served?
Waiter:	Right away. I'll Russia over to a table. What'll you Havre?
Customer:	I don't care—whatever's hot. But can't Jamaica cook hurry?
Waiter:	Odessa good joke! But Alaska anyway.
Customer:	And I'll take a cup of Java, too. Could you put a Cuba sugar in it?
Waiter:	Hey, Sweden it yourself, buddy.
Customer:	Then you better call the Bosporus so I can complain. I hope he'll Kenya.
Waiter:	You sure Ararat!
Customer:	Samoa your jokes? Do you think all this arguing Alps business?
Waiter:	You Spain in the neck—go somewhere else for lunch.
Customer:	Well, Abyssinia later.

GEOGRAPHY RIDDLES
A world full of humor

What is the greatest surgical operation on record?

Lansing, Michigan.

What's the biggest moving job in the world?

Wheeling, West Virginia.

What state is round at both ends and high in the middle?

Ohio.

What country do you become on a cold morning?

Chile.

What state is an exclamation?

OH

What state is a number?

Tenn.

What's the cleanest state?

Wash.

What state is like a parent?

PA

What state saved Noah and the animals?

Ark.

What state has the best doctors?

MD

What state has the most metal?

Ore.

What state has the worst health?

Ill.

What state is a grain?

RI (rye).

What state is self-centered?

ME

WHAT DID DELAWARE?
More geography funnies

What did Delaware?

She wore her New Jersey.

What did Idaho?

She hoed her Maryland.

What did Tennessee?

She saw what Arkansas.

What state has four eyes but can't see?

Mississippi.

Which is the friendliest state?

O-hi-o.

If the green house is on the right side of the road and the red house is on the left side of the road, where is the white house?

In Washington, D.C.

Who should you call when you find Chicago, Ill?

Baltimore, MD.

Where do cows go on vacation?

Moo York.

Can you name the capital of every state in the union in less than fifteen seconds?

Yes. Washington, D.C.

STORIES WITH HOLES
A classic game of strange stories

Choose someone to be the Quizmaster. She should read one of the stories below out loud, then read the answer to herself. (Answers on page 111.) Each of the stories is missing some important piece of information that explains the strange situation. The other players must guess the piece of information that will explain the story. Players take turns asking the Quizmaster yes or no questions about the situation. If the question isn't important to the solution of the puzzle, the Quizmaster should answer "It doesn't matter." For example, in the first story, the Quizmaster would answer these questions as follows:

"Is what the man screams important?" "No."

"Do the two men know one another?" "It doesn't matter."

"Is the man happy when he leaves?" "Yes."

The first person to fill the hole in the story reads out a new one, and the game begins again. When there are no more stories, people can take turns making up their own stories with holes.

Story 1: A man walks into a luncheonette and says something to the man behind the counter. The man behind the counter screams loudly at the man, who says "Thank you" and leaves.

Story 2: Marie wanted to get into an exclusive club, but she needed to know the password, so she listened as other members entered. When the first person knocked, the doorman said, "Twelve." The first person answered, "Six," and was let inside. A second person knocked, and the doorman said, "Six." The second person replied, "Three," and was let inside. So Marie walked up and knocked on the door, and the doorman said, "Ten." Marie answered, "Five," and was not let in. What should Marie have said?

Story 3: A man living in a high-rise apartment building has an odd way of using the elevator. Every day, he leaves his apartment on the twentieth floor and takes the elevator all the way down to the first floor, then leaves the building. Every night, he returns from work, takes the elevator to the fifteenth floor, then walks up the rest of the way. Why?

Story 4: Jack and Jill lie in a puddle of water on the floor in the middle of a room, next to a table surrounded by broken glass. What happened?

Story 5: In the big tent, the music stopped and a man fell into a giant net. What happened?

Story 6: A woman driving an eighteen-wheel truck is stopped in front of a bridge because her truck is one inch too tall to fit under it. A child gives the trucker some simple advice, which allows the truck to fit under the bridge. What does the child say?

Story 7: While a man is changing a flat tire, he unscrews the four nuts holding on the tire. While changing the tire, he accidentally drops the nuts into a sewer grating and can't retrieve them. He sits for a little while, then figures out a way to put the spare tire on and drive home safely. What does he do?

Story 8: Sam the coin collector is working at his store when a man comes in and offers to sell him an ancient, valuable coin. "Look right here," he tells Sam. "It says in ancient Greek, '56 B.C.'" Sam doesn't buy the coin. Why?

Story 9: A scientist gets a call from an inventor who says he has found a solution so strong that it dissolves any substance instantly. When the scientist says she is interested in seeing a sample, the inventor tells him he'll bring a few cups right over. The scientist says, "No thanks," and hangs up. Why?

ANSWERS

Pages 78–79:

1. Alabama, Alaska, Arizona, California, Florida, Georgia, Indiana, Iowa, Louisiana, Minnesota, Montana, Nebraska, Nevada, North Carolina, North Dakota, Oklahoma, Pennsylvania, South Carolina, South Dakota, Virginia, and West Virginia

2. Florida, Idaho, Iowa, Maine, New York, Texas, Utah, Vermont, and Wyoming

3. Alabama, Alaska, Hawaii, Indiana, Iowa, Kansas, Mississippi, Tennessee, and Utah

4. a. California; b. Florida; c. Rhode Island; d. Hawaii; e. Delaware; f. Missouri; g. Nevada; h. Alaska; i. Kentucky; j. Arizona; k. Massachusetts; l. New Mexico; m. Alabama.

5. Connecticut, Delaware, Florida, Georgia, Maine, Maryland, Massachusetts, New Hampshire, New Jersey, New York, North Carolina, Rhode Island, South Carolina, and Virginia

6. California, Oregon, and Washington

Pages 108–110:

Story 1: The man had the hiccups.

Story 2: The password is based on the number of letters in the word the doorman said; Marie should have said, "Three," as there are three letters in the word *ten*.

Story 3: The man is too short to reach the button for the twentieth floor and can reach only up to the fifteenth-floor button. The first-floor button is located lower, so he can reach that.

Story 4: Jack and Jill are fish. The glass and water came from their fishbowl, which fell and shattered on the floor.

Story 5: The man was a blindfolded tightrope walker who used the music to tell him when it was safe to step onto the platform. When the music stopped too early, he thought he was in front of the platform, stepped forward, and fell.

Story 6: The child told the trucker to let enough air out of the tires to drop the truck one inch.

Story 7: He removes one nut from each of the other three wheels, giving him three nuts for each wheel, which makes the car safe to drive until he can replace the missing nuts.

Story 8: They didn't know in what we call 56 B.C. that Christ would be born, so they couldn't have marked the coins this way. The term "B.C." was invented later.

Story 9: If the solution dissolves anything instantly, there's no container that could hold it. The inventor must be lying.

SONGS

FAMILY JUKEBOX
Hours of fun that won't cost you a single quarter

1. The first player names a theme word that might be found in a song title. *Love,* *morning,* and *ride* are all good examples.

2. The next player names a song title containing the theme word. She must then sing the first verse of the song.

3. Play continues with each player naming a new song title and singing the first verse. When a player cannot name a song title, he is out.

4. The last player remaining is the winner. She names a new theme word, and the game begins again!

The point of this game is to sing and share songs, so players can sing the whole song (or whatever portion they know) rather than the first verse. And if you know the words, sing along!

THE ANTS GO MARCHING

ground   to   get   out   of   the   rain.   Boom!   Boom!   Boom!

3. The ants go marching three by three, hurrah, hurrah.
   The ants go marching three by three, hurrah, hurrah.
   The ants go marching three by three; the little one stops to climb a tree,
   And they all go marching down into the ground to get out of the rain.
   Boom! Boom! Boom!

4. The ants go marching four by four, hurrah, hurrah.
   The ants go marching four by four, hurrah, hurrah.
   The ants go marching four by four; the little one stops to shut the door,
   And they all go marching down into the ground to get out of the rain.
   Boom! Boom! Boom!

5. The ants go marching five by five, hurrah, hurrah.
   The ants go marching five by five, hurrah, hurrah.
   The ants go marching five by five; the little one stops to take a dive,
   And they all go marching down into the ground to get out of the rain.
   Boom! Boom! Boom!

6. The ants go marching six by six, hurrah, hurrah.
   The ants go marching six by six, hurrah, hurrah.
   The ants go marching six by six; the little one stops to pick up sticks,
   And they all go marching down into the ground to get out of the rain.
   Boom! Boom! Boom!

7. The ants go marching seven by seven, hurrah, hurrah.
   The ants go marching seven by seven, hurrah, hurrah.
   The ants go marching seven by seven; the little one stops to pray to heaven,
   And they all go marching down into the ground to get out of the rain.
   Boom! Boom! Boom!

8. The ants go marching eight by eight, hurrah, hurrah.
   The ants go marching eight by eight, hurrah, hurrah.
   The ants go marching eight by eight; the little one stops to close the gate,
   And they all go marching down into the ground to get out of the rain.
   Boom! Boom! Boom!

9. The ants go marching nine by nine, hurrah, hurrah.
   The ants go marching nine by nine, hurrah, hurrah.
   The ants go marching nine by nine; the little one stops to spend a dime,
   And they all go marching down into the ground to get out of the rain.
   Boom! Boom! Boom!

10. The ants go marching ten by ten, hurrah, hurrah.
    The ants go marching ten by ten, hurrah, hurrah.
    The ants go marching ten by ten; the little one stops to say,
    (shouted) "THE END!"

IF YOU'RE HAPPY

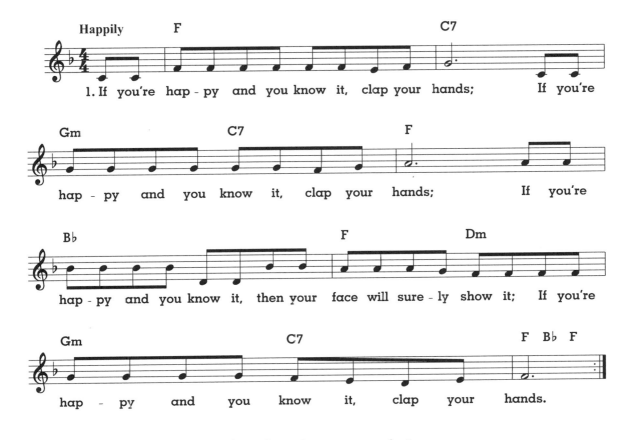

2. If you're happy and you know it, stomp your feet;
   If you're happy and you know it, stomp your feet;
   If you're happy and you know it, then your face will surely show it;
   If you're happy and you know it, stomp your feet.

3. If you're happy and you know it, say "AMEN!"
   If you're happy and you know it, say "AMEN!"
   If you're happy and you know it, then your face will surely show it;
   If you're happy and you know it, say "AMEN!"

   Now make up some verses of your own!

THE LIMERICK SONG

Lively

Chorus:

Aye - aye - aye - aye _____ In
Chi - na they nev - er grow chil - ly. _____ So
sing me an - oth - er verse That's worse than the first verse; Make
sure that it's fool - ish and sil - ly. _____

Fine

Verse:

1. A   tu - tor   who   toot - ed   the   flute _____ Tried to
2. There was   an   old   man from Pe - ru _____ Who

C7						F				F7
tu - tor	two	toot - ers	to	toot.				Said the
dreamed he	was	eat - ing	his	shoe.				When he

Bb					F	A7	Dm
two	to	the	tu - tor,	"Is it	tough - er	to	toot, or	To
woke	in	a	fright	In the	dark	of the	night,	He

G7		C7		F		(to Chorus)
tu - tor	two	toot - ers	to	toot?"	
found	it	was	per - fect - ly	true.	

Verse:

3. There once was a young fellow of Perth
   Who was born on the day of his birth.
   He was married, they say,
   On his wife's wedding day,
   And he died when he quitted the earth. *Chorus:*

4. A man who was dining at Crewe
   Found quite a large mouse in his stew.
   Said the waiter, "Don't shout
   And wave it about
   Or the rest will be wanting one too!" *Chorus:*

Now add some wacky limericks of your own!

A STATELY SONG

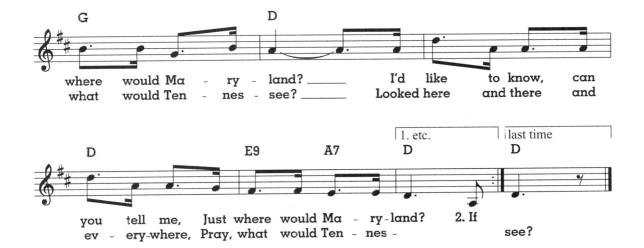

where would Ma - ry - land? _____ I'd like to know, can
what would Ten - nes - see? _____ Looked here and there and

you tell me, Just where would Ma - ry - land? 2. If
ev - ery-where, Pray, what would Ten - nes - see?

1. etc.   last time

3. I looked out of the window and
   Saw Orry on the lawn.
   He's not there now, and who can tell
   Just where has Oregon?
   Oh, where has Oregon?
   Oh, where has Oregon?
   He's not there now, and who can tell
   Just where has Oregon?

4. Two girls were quarreling one day
   With gardening tools, and so
   I said, "My dears, let Mary rake,
   And just let Idaho.
   Oh, just let Idaho, oh, just let Idaho;"
   I said, "My dears, let Mary rake,
   And just let Idaho!"

   Try to think up your own punny state verses and sing them!

BINGO

Sing all the way through the first time. On the second time through, sing faster and clap instead of saying "B." On the third time, sing even faster and clap twice for "B-I," and so on, until you clap only for the word *BINGO*.

THE PEANUT SONG

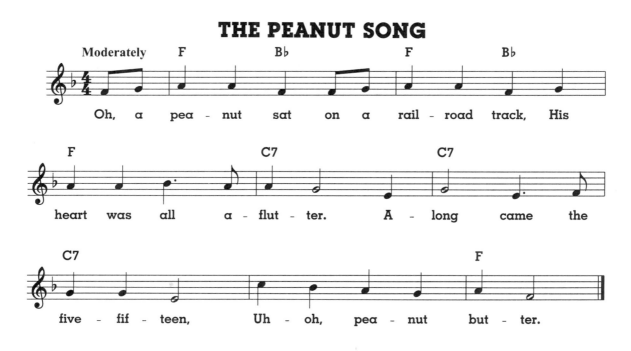

I'VE BEEN WORKING ON THE RAILROAD

OH, SUSANNA!

Verse:

2. It rained all day the night I left, the weather it was dry.
   The sun so hot I froze myself, Susanna don't you cry. *Chorus:*

3. I had a dream the other night, when everything was still.
   I thought I saw Susanna a-comin' down the hill. *Chorus:*

4. The red, red rose was in her hand, the tear was in her eye.
   I said, "I come from Dixie Land, Susanna don't you cry." *Chorus:*

THE WHEELS ON THE BUS

3. The wipers on the bus go, "Swish, swish, swish,
   Swish, swish, swish, swish, swish, swish."
   The wipers on the bus go, "Swish, swish, swish,"
   All the way to town.

4. The driver of the bus goes, "Shhh, shhh, shhh,
   Shhh, shhh, shhh, shhh, shhh, shhh."
   The driver of the bus goes, "Shhh, shhh, shhh,"
   All the way to town.

   Make up your own bus noises — the weirder, the better!